THE
Archive Photographs
SERIES

ROCHDALE

So that's how they did it! Piano removals using a block and tackle at Old Market Chambers, Yorkshire Street, c.1920. Laurel and Hardy could have taken a few tips from Sam Sharpe, a railway carter from Smithy Bridge (wearing the 'pot' hat) and his colleagues. The premises, across the Roebuck Entry from the Yorkshire Bank, were occupied by Clement W. Coomer, a stockbroker, in 1916, although they subsequently became the home of the GPO Club. And the horse's name? 'Dolly' of course.

THE
Archive Photographs
SERIES

ROCHDALE

Compiled by
Pam Godman

ROCHDALE
METROPOLITAN BOROUGH
COUNCIL

CHALFORD

First published 1996
Copyright © Pam Godman, 1996

The Chalford Publishing Company
St Mary's Mill, Chalford,
Stroud, Gloucestershire, GL6 8NX

ISBN 0 7524 0382 6

Typesetting and origination by
The Chalford Publishing Company
Printed in Great Britain by
Redwood Books, Trowbridge

Contents

Acknowledgements

Rochdale Local Studies Library would like to thank all those who have made this volume possible, especially the photographers, both known and unknown, amateur or professional, whose images appear, and members of the public who have been generous in loaning or donating their prints to the Library in order to help to preserve the town's past for future generations to see. With particular acknowledgements to: Akzo Chemie Ltd; Mr Allen; Clifford Ashton; Mrs F. Broxup; Mr Buckley; Mr F. Butterworth; Mr P. Cryer; Mr Edwards; David Grayson of Littleborough Historical and Archaeological Society; The Chief Constable, Greater Manchester Police; Mr T. Harvey; Holroyds (Renold Group); Mrs J. Metcalfe; Mrs Schofield; Mrs Tuck; the Watson Family and Mr L. Wild. The help and support given by Joy Hopwood, Joan Kelly and Chris Watkins was invaluable, and very special thanks go to David Dunton for his care and patience in the processing of our photographs.

Introduction

This volume of images, documenting the changing face of Rochdale and the surrounding area, has been assembled from the excellent photographic archive held by Rochdale's Local Studies Library. Through the camera's eye, we are offered glimpses of Rochdale's recent past, with images of people, places and events frozen against the relentless flow of time.

Old photographs come to light among family papers as snapshots and formal groups. We find them within business and official archives, in newspapers and as picture postcards. Whatever their source, they are a treasure trove of images, captured by both amateur and professional photographers, which offer a visual documentation of our town's recent history, augmenting the information supplied by written records.

Rochdale's recorded history began with an entry in the Domesday Book of 1086, when William the Conqueror had the country surveyed for the purpose of assessing taxation. By 1251 the town was important enough to have been granted a market charter, with the right to hold weekly markets on Wednesdays, and an annual fair in October each year. At the same time, Rochdale was at the hub of one of the largest ecclesiastical parishes in the country.

Over the following centuries Rochdale grew slowly and steadily until in 1724, Daniel Defoe described it as 'a good market town of late much improved in the woollen market.' Sited on the border between Lancashire and Yorkshire, Rochdale was, indeed, well placed to take advantage of the growing woollen trade, with a network of packhorse tracks criss-crossing the moors like a web between the various towns and villages. Later on came the privately financed turnpikes, intended to ease the lot of the traveller, but charging tolls for their upkeep. Blackstone Edge (Old Road), linking Rochdale and Halifax, was the first in the area to be turnpiked, in 1735.

In the late 1700s Rochdale was described as being 'remarkable for many wealthy merchants,' and had several 'manufactures' where mechanisation was beginning to creep in, as forward-looking men utilized the inventions of Arkwright, Hargreaves and Crompton. Mechanisation, however, with its bigger and more complex machines, required power as well as larger buildings and thus the landscape of the town and the rhythm of people's lives began to change.

Spurred on by expanding trade, Rochdale's merchants realised that there was a need for better communication links and local men like Richard Townley of Belfield and Colonel Beswicke Royds of Pike House at Littleborough, proposed the construction of Rochdale Canal in 1766, although it was to be thirty-eight years before their plans came to fruition when the canal was finally opened throughout in 1804. A mere thirty-seven years later, in 1841, the Manchester to Leeds railway was completed, presenting a major challenge to canal traffic and profits.

By 1844, when the Rochdale Equitable Pioneer's Co-operative Society began to trade,

Rochdale had emerged as a busy industrial town, with textiles, coal mining and engineering amongst the most important industries. But there was a price. Rapid urbanisation was to transform the appearance of the town dramatically, and the lives of its inhabitants drastically, as factories, foundries, and above all, row upon row of terraced houses were built to accommodate industrial processes and the influx of people who served them.

During 1856, when photography was in its infancy, Rochdale was incorporated as a Borough, with a population estimated at 34,545. Jacob Bright, brother of John, served as the town's first mayor. Over the next fifty years the Town Council paved and lit the streets, developed water supplies, improved sewage and refuse disposal (making money from the sale of Rochdale Manure which was produced from sewage) and demolished slum areas. They took over the supply of gas and electricity, built schools, developed tramways, acquired parks and public gardens, built the library and later an art gallery and museum, partially covered the River Roch, and erected the magnificent gothic style Town Hall, which was opened on 27 September 1871 by the Mayor, George Leach Ashworth. Other duties included the running of the police and fire services, plus the development of a public health programme.

Throughout all the industrialisation and amidst newly awakened municipal pride, the people of Rochdale and the surrounding areas continued with the rhythms of their lives. Schooldays came and went and working lives were punctuated by holidays, often all too brief. There were visits to the theatre, music halls and later on, cinemas; trips to the country or seaside, fun at the fairground or walks in the park. People gossiped on doorsteps, shopped, attended church or chapel, joined in the Whit Walks and gathered in huge crowds to watch civic processions. They lived through good times and bad times, war and peace, and often, it seems, there was someone around with a camera to record an event and attract a crowd.

Photographs are commonplace today when almost everyone has access to a camera to record family occasions for themselves. We are surrounded by images in newspapers, magazines and books; they adorn hoardings, exhorting us to buy this or that and are recognised as powerful persuaders. Above all, they enter our homes via the television screen, bringing us news from the other side of the world as it occurs. How different and magical the photograph must have appeared to our nineteenth-century forbears, and what a telling tool it became for instigating social change.

Newgate, photographed by T. Harvey, around 1970.

One
Town Centre Changes

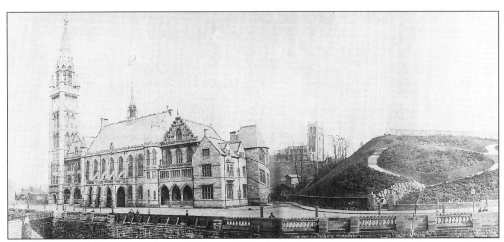

Rochdale's magnificent, gothic style Town Hall, designed by W.H. Crossland, photographed in 1874.

The Town Hall Square in 1893 when Charles Kershaw's Central Corn Mill, demolished in 1934, stood below the Parish Church and buildings clustered up against the Church Steps. The Town Hall, completed in 1871 at a cost of £160,000, stands on the right of the Square. In this view we see the new 190 foot high tower designed by Alfred Waterhouse, the architect of Manchester Town Hall. This replaced the original 240 foot high tower which was destroyed by fire on 10 April 1883.

Looking north across the Town Hall Square from the recently planted St Chad's Gardens, c.1905. The Technical School stands on the right, behind the original Flying Horse Hotel which faced onto the Square.

Hansom cabs waiting for fares on the Esplanade, c.1910.

Amen Corner, or the Great House, in 1908, shortly before it was demolished to make way for Newgate. In 1565 the Great House was occupied by Robert Gartside, but in later years it was used variously as a public house, religious meeting place and then finally, as advertised on the wall in this picture, as a lodging house.

Wheelpit Court and the River Roch, c.1909. Like the Great House, this area stood in the way of Newgate, and suffered the same fate. The Hippodrome, which can be seen behind the buildings, survived. Just as well, since it had been built only a year earlier, in 1908.

Orchard or Manor House, c.1897. Built early in the eighteenth century the Orchard was acquired by Simon Dearden in 1745, becoming known as the Manor House following the family's purchase of the Manor of Rochdale from the poet Lord Byron in 1823. As the Orchard was a recruiting office in the First World War it seems fitting that the site was chosen for the war memorial.

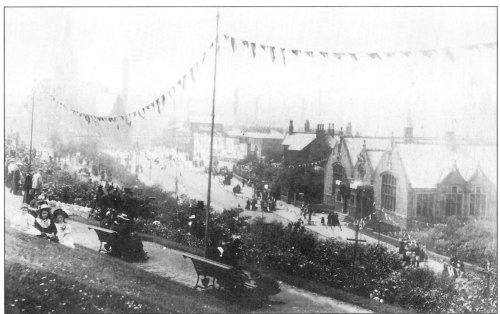

Rochdale Central Library pictured during the celebrations for Queen Victoria's Jubilee in 1897, prior to the building of the Art Gallery and Museum extensions. Trinity Presbyterian church stands on the left and numerous mill chimneys crowd the background.

Children pose on the Church Steps in 1900. Much earlier, on 12 July 1759, St Chad's churchwarden recorded that 'it is agreed that Thomas Kershaw (sexton) is to have 5/- (25p) a year for keeping the Church Steps clean.' It was money hard earned, for there are no fewer than 122 stone steps, built from stone quarried on Blackstone Edge. To the right of the steps were Leyland Chambers, the premises of Worth and Worth, solicitors. These buildings were demolished in 1934, whilst the former 'red light' area, between the infamous Gank and Church Lane, to the left of the steps, had been cleared of its 'houses of ill-repute' and slum dwellings in 1886.

14

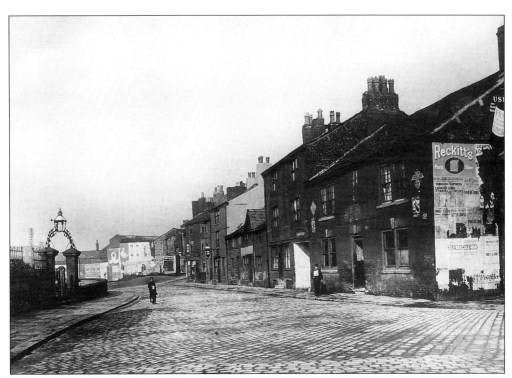

Church Stile in 1895 with a full complement of houses, shops and public houses. On the left, in the churchyard, are the stocks, reputedly last used in 1822 to confine a Rochdalian named Bill Pod.

St Chad's Parish Church, viewed from the vicarage gardens in 1893. Although it is likely that a church has occupied this site since Saxon times, the earliest written records date from 1194 when the vicar was one Geoffrey the Elder. This image shows the effects of major alterations in the late nineteenth century, when the tower was heightened (but lost its clock) the chancel was extended and the porch replaced.

Steam tram at the bottom of Drake Street, c.1900. Little changed, except for the names: James Duckworth's Temperence Hotel became the Co-op's Fashion Corner in 1922, and now houses the Council's Treasurer's Department.

An open-topped tram climbing Drake Street in 1904, almost opposite a branch of Boots the Chemist's. The street was named after Thomas Drake, Vicar of Rochdale between 1790 and 1819. Ann Street and Richard Street were named after his children.

Yorkshire Street in 1890, showing the Blue Bell Inn, now Yates', with a barrel over the door and a cartload of 'shoddy' outside, destined, no doubt, for one of the mills in Baillie Street.

The Walk in 1890. Walter Vavasour, son of a local woollen merchant, is credited with the building of the whole block in the early 1800s.

17

Rochdale's Top Market in 1905, looking towards Toad Lane. In 1822 a newly formed Market Company bought all market rights from the Lord of the Manor, establishing a new market in the area between Yorkshire Street, Cheetham Street, Toad Lane and Blackwater Street.

Rochdale's original Market Hall, better known as the 'inside market,' c.1910. Built in 1824, the Market Hall burned down in 1937 but was rebuilt within two years, opening its doors once more on 18 December 1939.

Bottom Market, between Lord Street and Toad Lane, c.1900. Edwin Waugh, the celebrated dialect writer, was born in a cottage on the site of the Old Clock Face in 1817.

Yorkshire Street around 1925 with market stalls outside King's ironmongers, now Lloyds bank. Clifton's tobacconists stands on the corner of Lord Street, in the building occupied for many years by Bowden's sweetshop, while Saville's Ladies' Costumiers occupies a corner of the Walk.

Toad Lane in the early summer of 1968 showing market stalls, Hopwood's pet shop and the Market Inn, which was licensed only for beer. This photograph was taken by Mr Tuck who owned Brook's Stores on the right of the picture.

Rochdale Cattle Market, c.1910. Cattle markets were held on the Holme, opposite the Town Hall, between 1877 and 1951. Earlier livestock markets were held in Church Lane.

St Mary's Gate in 1959, prior to demolition work for the inner ring road. Thomas's chemists stands on the corner of Hanging Road, while Clover Street chapel, often dubbed the Pioneer's Chapel, can be seen on the corner of Spotland Road behind the No.10 bus which ran between Turf Hill and Syke. For many years the chapel building was used as a Sunday school.

Fording the Roch, c.1780. Taken from a painting originally in the possession of the Royds family, this image depicts the seeds of industrialisation, with cloth being fulled in a leat branching off the river and a forge in use behind the large house which still stands at the bottom of Drake Street, now known as 'Bojangles'. In 1780 the house belonged to Thomas Smith, a wealthy woollen merchant. Later on it became a school, then the Wellington Hotel.

The Walk Footbridge, with the Wellington Bridge in the background, around 1900. Perhaps the greatest change to affect the landscape of the town centre was the covering of the River Roch by what has been claimed to be the widest bridge in the world. In 1903 the council unveiled its plans to cover the Roch between the Butts and South Parade, thus creating space for a central tramway terminus with wide thoroughfares, hiding the then heavily polluted river from sight.

Looking towards the Town Hall in 1902, prior to the covering.

Looking eastwards from the bottom of the Walk, c.1904. This image shows the work involved in strengthening the river bed and controlling the flow at a cost of £4,000. Prior to completion the Walk Footbridge, still a feature in this picture, had to be removed.

Spectacular weight tests were made on completion of the first phase of the covering in 1904, with massive tonnage rolled onto the finished roadway.

Town centre, c.1930. Work on covering the river spanned a period of twenty-three years. The second phase, between Yorkshire Street and Newgate, was completed in 1910, but it was to be 1923, five years after the end of the First World War, before phase three, between Newgate and the Holme, now the site of the police station, was finished. Finally, in January 1926, when the section between the old Wellington Bridge and Weir Street was opened, the bridge attained its full width, eventually gaining a place in the Guinness Book of Records. The river covering has recently been the focus of intense interest, as the repair works of 1995/1996 once more revealed the graceful lines of the old Rochdale Bridge.

Two
Roundabout Rochdale

Ye Three Cups Coffee House and Temperence Hotel, Sudden, c.1910.

St Aiden's Mission at Marland Old Road was designed by Edgar Wood, the Middleton architect and opened in 1897. When the present St Aiden's church on Manchester Road was consecrated in 1915, the Mission became a Sunday school.

Castleton Hall in 1890 when it had been purchased by Thomas Champness and turned into a training centre for Methodist preachers and missionaries, known as the Joyful News Training Home. Dating from around 1542, when Robert Holt of Stubley purchased the estate, Castleton Hall was one of the most impressive buildings in the area. Its classically styled south wing was added by Samuel Cheetham in the eighteenth century.

Onlookers at the demolition of Castleton Hall in 1920 when it was knocked down to make way for the Kilworth Street housing estate.

Castleton Cricket Ground, c.1880. John Jackson captured this image of players and spectators waiting for the groundsman to complete his preparation of the pitch. Four players from the Castleton team were chosen for the Lancashire XI in June 1885: F. Taylor, W.E. and R.C. Leach and C. Haigh.

An empty looking Queensway in 1925 with Arrow Mill in the distance on the left, Ensor and Crest Mills in the centre, and the enormous bulk of Dunlop's on the right.

Oldham Road at Lowerplace, c.1910. A branch of James Duckworth's grocery chain stands at the junction of Oldham Road and Kings Road, in the middle of what is now Kingsway. The barber's shop on the right of the picture belonged to John Ellis, the public hangman.

Houses at Cronkeyshaw, photographed on the occasion of Queen Victoria's Diamond Jubilee, 21 June 1897. An inscription over the door of the house with the porch reads JST 1734, which refers to John Taylor, a merchant from Toad Lane. By 1925 the whole row was known as Chadwick Houses.

Shawclough Road, c.1890 looking towards Healey with the old Pioneers' store on the right, in front of the entrance to the Rochdale Asbestos and India Rubber Works. (See also p. 53).

Horsecarrs Coffee Tavern, c.1905. Built in the mid 1860s by Thomas Watson, the tavern stood at the entrance to his silk mill in Shawclough. By 1905 the building was being used by Rochdale Electric Company which was founded and owned by Thomas's son, William. Products included dynamos, light fittings and electric motors. (See also p. 43).

Gathering in the hay from Hamer Hall fields, c.1890. Everyone lent a hand at haytime, including groups of Irish labourers who travelled from farm to farm.

Belfield Hall. c.1890. Belonging amongst others, to the Belfields, Butterworths and Richard Townley, the old hall was built with a quadrangle, or inner courtyard. Richard Townley, who had been Steward to Alexander Butterworth, built the fine Georgian frontage seen above, in 1752. Yearsley's Frozen Food warehouse now occupies the site.

Whit Friday procession at Smallbridge in 1905. Everyone dressed in their best for the Whit Walks, usually an occasion for new clothes or, at the very least, new trimmings for your hat.

The Boat Inn, c.1900. One of the strangest of Rochdale's long vanished public houses was 'Uncle Tom's Cabin,' popularly known as the Boat Inn. Hauled out of the canal in 1841 after many years of plying trade as a passenger boat between Heywood and Bluepits, Castleton, the barge was beached on Belfield Road, not far from Belfield Hall. For many years the licencee was Thomas Butterworth, known as 'Tom o'th'Boat', possibly giving rise to the name 'Uncle Tom's Cabin.' He may even have been the Butterworth who purchased, relocated and transformed the barge by building sloping brick sides over the deck, with porthole windows to preserve a nautical air. The large board at the front of the picture listed the tolls chargeable to traffic on Belfield Road. These were collected by Thomas Butterworth, as toll keeper, and included receipts from colliers' carts. The Boat lost its licence on grounds of redundancy in 1909 and was broken up in the same year.

Inside the Boat Inn, c.1900. A rare glimpse into the interior shows us some of the regulars at the Boat.

Beer deliveries at the Green Man Inn, Hurstead, c.1905. Good 'baitings' for horses are advertised alongside wines, spirits and ale.

Milnrow Road at Firgrove, c.1910. Belfield's 'Tin Church,' which can be seen on the left, was built in 1905 to serve the people of Belfield and Firgrove. The building was purchased from Isaac Dixon of Liverpool at a cost of £900, opening in November 1905. It was replaced by the present stone built St Ann's Church in 1913.

Strolling, listening to the band, or dancing the day away; you could take your pick in Ashworth Valley at Eastertime in 1906.

Naden Dairy Farm, Norden, c.1910. Benjamin Butterworth, who farmed at Naden in the mid nineteenth century, was awarded Manchester Agricultural Society's Special Prize in 1850 to indicate their admiration for his efforts in producing a crop of swedish turnips 'in the high and ungenial district in which his farm is situated.'

Dr Dam Cottages, off Greenbooth Road in Norden, c.1900.

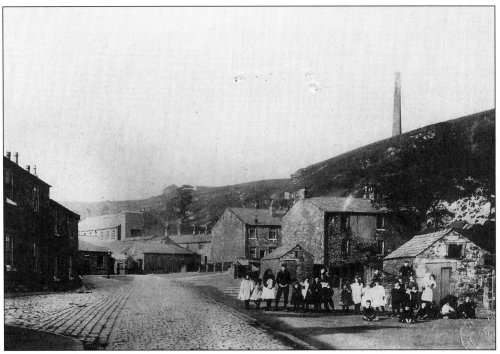

Greenbooth Village and Mill, c.1930. Both village and mill sank beneath 700 million gallons of water when Greenbooth Reservoir was completed in 1961.

Three
Focussed on People

William Tatham, textile machinery manufacturer, pictured with his family at Sparrow Hill in 1875.

A daguerreotype of John Bright MP, probably dating from the late 1840s. Bright was a Quaker and millowner who is perhaps best remembered for his part in the campaign to repeal the Corn Laws, which were finally abolished in 1846.

Philip Fray, c.1856, here looking somewhat the worse for wear and perhaps nervous of the camera! This early example of portraiture is reputedly an image of one of the town's watercarriers.

Fourteen of the original Rochdale Pioneers, photographed in 1865 by John Jackson. These men were amongst the twenty eight who opened a Co-operative Trading Society in Toad Lane, Rochdale, on 21 December 1844, where they sold wholesome, unadulterated food at reasonable prices to society members. Their success, that led eventually to the worldwide Co-operative Movement, was based on their principles. These included: one member, one vote; equality of the sexes amongst membership; that only pure provisions should be sold, in full weight and measure, and perhaps most famously, the allocation of 'divi' (dividend) to members, guaranteeing that all profits were divided pro rata depending upon the amount of purchases made by individual members.

Shawmoss Farm, c.1880. Robert Hutchinson, dressed in the light suit, farmed eighteen acres at Shawmoss, just off Wildhouse Lane in Milnrow. He is pictured here with his wife, (kneeling with a baby on her lap), other members of his family, neighbours and even the animals, at some long forgotten celebration.

Edwin Waugh, c.1888. Popularly known as Rochdale's Prince of Dialect Poets, Waugh was born on 29 January 1817. His many books include *Lancashire Sketches* and *Factory Folk*, with perhaps his most famous poem being *Come Whoam to thi' Childer and Me*. He is seen here on board a friend's yacht, the *Hesperia*, during a cruise around the Scottish Isles.

Jimmy Gartside of Milnrow, smoking a clay pipe, c.1896. Jimmy, known locally as 'Irish Jimmy', lived in a cottage with his mother, Irish Hannah, at Butterworth Hall. On her demise Hannah is said to have caused two controversies. Was she, or was she not, a centenarian, and when did she last have a wash? Jimmy did contract work for local farmers as a 'muck spreader,' ie. he charged the farmers per meadow spread. His dog, pictured beside him, was a trailhound who gloried in the name Clonkalong.

Above: Members of the Watson family gathered together in 1905 to enjoy an Edwardian summer's afternoon in the garden of Horsecarrs, complete with croquet on the lawn.

Opposite: Times change! Pictured in the grounds of Horsecarrs in 1916 these employees of the Rochdale Electric Company, owned by Thomas Watson's son, were engaged in grenade manufacture at the Shawclough Coffee Tavern. (See also p. 30).

Thomas Watson of Horsecarrs, Shawclough, c.1885. Born in 1823, Watson was a silk manufacturer and hatter, MP for Ilkeston in Derbyshire and benefactor to the people of Rochdale giving, among other things, a building and funds to establish the Infirmary on Redcross Street in 1883. One of a family of seventeen children he began work at the age of eleven, eventually moving to Rochdale where he was to prosper from his hard work, inventive skills and undoubted business acumen.

Dressed to kill in 1903! The Scott sisters of Stubley New Hall, Littleborough, decked out in frills and flowers for a ball at Pike House where Katherine recalled dancing on a stone flagged floor. Photographed by their brother Leslie, with Mrs Hoard, the eldest sister, seated and suitably serious, while Florence, standing next to Katherine, the youngest, is laughing and obviously excited at the prospect of the dance.

Huge crowds gathered in the Town Hall Square on 23 June 1911 to watch the start of the Civic Parade marking the coronation of King George V and Queen Mary. A few daring individuals, including ladies in their long skirts and large picture hats, claimed uninterrupted views from the roof of the Flying Horse Hotel, demolished in June 1923, and the adjacent building. The present Flying Horse Hotel dates from 1926. In addition to the Civic Parade, there were bonfires at Healey, Cronkeyshaw, Buersil and Tunshill, while Alderman Turner chose to mark the occasion by opening the extension to Falinge Park: his gift to the town.

Arthur Greenoff and some of his workmen in the firm's yard on Livsey Street in 1915. Greenoff and Shaw were a coach and carrying firm who were contracted to transport locally produced munitions during the First World War. Cyril Shaw later spent some time at the front as an ambulance driver. Arthur Greenoff is seated on the right, below the cart. (See also p. 92).

Ellen Wallace, c.1915. Nicknamed 'Nell Racker,' Ellen was famed throughout the area as a midwife, herbalist, healer and fortune teller. Some also whispered that she was an abortionist, although this was never confirmed. She is pictured with her grandson in the doorway of Belfield Cottage.

Annie Cragg, one of Rochdale's first postwomen, c.1916. The First World War brought many new employment opportunities for women in both industry and public services. Annie, pictured here in uniform, had a postal round which included the Manchester Road and Merefield Street areas of Rochdale.

Beamers at Sandiford's Victoria Mill on Ramsay Street, c.1921.

Children and their mothers pose for the camera in Grove Street in 1930. The poverty and hardship which were the hallmark of life for many ordinary people in the thirties can be clearly seen in the dress of the group. Many of the children appear to be wearing 'hand-me-downs', while some are without socks and poorly shod. Still, having your photograph taken was an exciting event although perhaps a little overwhelming for two of the little boys on the front row.

Gracie Fields' visit to Rochdale on 3 March 1933 when she tried her hand at shoe repairs in the Handicraft Centre for Unemployed Men which had been opened by the People's Service Guild in 1932. Born above her grandmother's chip shop on Molesworth Street on 9 January 1898, Gracie was to sing and clown her way to international stardom until, at one time, she was the highest paid movie star in the world. Certainly Rochdale's best known personality, Gracie, born Grace Stansfield, began her career with a talent show at the Rochdale Hippodrome, coming joint first at the age of ten and winning 10/6d (52p) which was almost half the average weekly wage of a millworker at that time.

Children from St Ann's church, Belfield, parading their banner along Rathbone Street at Whitsuntide, c.1930.

Mrs Allen and her son, caught on film outside their fish and chip shop on Lord Street, Rochdale, in 1935.

The Chapel Choir, Bagslate Moor Methodist church, photographed by W.T. Carter in 1937.

Members of Rochdale's Auxilliary Fire Service, stationed at Norden in 1942. Seen here on excercise with a Minorca pump, were Michael Howe, in the centre, with Norman Jagger on the right.

Everyone lent a hand in the Dig for Victory campaign during the Second World War, helping to eke out and improve the basic food rations.

Rochdale people crowded into the town centre on 2 June 1948 to see Queen Elizabeth, now the Queen Mother, on her visit to Rochdale.

Four
People at Work

Rochdale Asbestos Company, c.1900. Asbestos was both spun and woven at the works for products which included asbestos mattresses!

Above: mill interior, probably Mitchell Hey, c.1890, showing reeling. This involved unwinding the spun yarn from cops or bobbins, which can be seen at the bottom of the machine frame, then rewinding it onto the revolving frame. This process produced skeins or hanks of cotton ready for bleaching, dying or sizing. Cops of cotton can be seen in one of the basket skips in the foreground.

Crest Ring Mill at March Barn, Castleton, c.1906. Women operatives still wore clogs to work in the cotton mills at that time for comfort and durability.

Billhead, Morningside Mills, c.1920, woollen mills with a difference. William Hastings and Sons of Morningside Mills, established in 1850, spun the wool of angora rabbits. This billhead illustrates the mills' impressive frontage on Crawford Street together with its canalside rear entrances, just along the towpath from Oldham Road.

roup @ Rydings Mill 1900
"DS WE WERE"

Above: halftimers pose for the camera outside Rydings Mill at Wardle in 1900.

Halftimers knelt to keep a sharp eye on the raising process during the manufacture of flannelette at Sam Heap's Spotland Bridge Mill, c.1910.

Halftimers at work in a Rochdale weaving shed, c.1900. Following the Education Act of 1870 all children were to receive compulsory education but many were subjected to the halftime system, particularly within the textile trades. Under this system, children aged between 10 and 14 years attended school for half the day and worked the other half. In 1892 the minimum age for working was raised to 11 years and in 1900, to 12 years, and, it must be said, that there was some parental opposition to the new exemptions. Halftimers started work at 6 am, attending school in the afternoon. On the following week they went to school in the morning and worked from 1 pm to 5.30 pm with a Saturday morning shift as well. Thus two children shared one job. Only with the Fisher Act of 1918, when exemption from fulltime education was banned, were the little halftimers finally released from their bondage. Perhaps we should also recall that children under 10 years old and often of 5 years or less were pressed into working for long hours in Britain's industries in the years before 1870.

TO MINERS, SINKERS, AND OTHERS.

TO BE LET,

BY TICKET,

At Small-Bridge Colliery, near Rochdale,

On Saturday, January 5th, 1839,

AT SIX O'CLOCK IN THE EVENING,

THE DRIVING OF A

TUNNEL,

Of about 70 yards in length, 4 feet wide, and 3 feet 6 inches high, at the aforesaid Colliery.

For further particulars, apply to Mr. James Turner, Small-Bridge, or at the said Colliery.

JONES & CROSSKILL, PRINTERS, ROCHDALE.

Notice advertising tunnelling work at Smallbridge Colliery, owned by James Dearden, in 1839. Under the agreement, all tools and materials were to be provided by the 'letters.' The 'takers' of the contract were to guarantee to work two shifts daily, of at least ten hours each, with penalties for any shift of less than ten hours. Edmund Hartley won the work on 7 January 1839, at a price of 16/- (80p) per yard.

A group of colliers from Norden where there were a number of pits, including Bagslate and Greenbooth, c.1912.

Butterworth Hall Colliery, Milnrow, c.1910. Coalmining was one of Rochdale's oldest industries, with 'colepittes' recorded at Littleborough and Falinge in 1580. By the mid nineteenth century the area boasted numerous pits including Butterworth Hall, which became the largest, employing around 300 men in 1912.

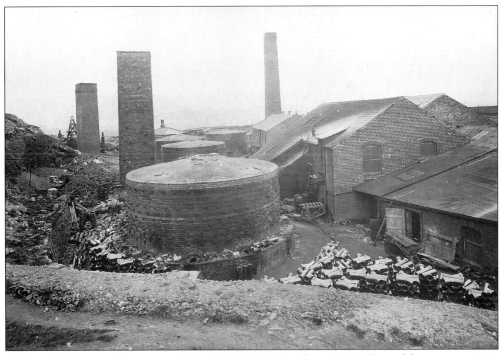

Ashworth's Starring Potteries and Fireclay Works, Dearnley, c.1909. Four of the company's six kilns are shown here as well as the machine houses, with the headgear of the claypit in the distance.

A rare glimpse of underground workings at Starring in 1909 showing two miners breaking up the clay ready for its removal to the surface. Blasting was used to loosen the clay as it was a very hard material.

Moulders and machinists at Starring Potteries in 1909. In the foreground a finished bend moulding is being eased out of a pressure moulding machine. The man on the right is scoring grooves around the inside of the top of a large mains sewer pipe to ensure a good purchase and strong, watertight joint when the pipes were cemented together.

Workmen at the Newhey Brick and Terracotta Works, Huddersfield Road, Newhey, c.1910.

Engineers and apprentices pictured at Holroyd's Whitehall Street Foundry in 1910.

Engineers on the shopfloor at Holroyd's Whitehall Street Foundry in 1910. Holroyd's acquired the Whitehall Street premises from John Petrie in 1906 after moving to Milnrow from Manchester in 1896. Rochdale has a long tradition of engineering, rooted in the skills of early millwrights, smiths, clockmakers and textile cardmakers and developed through the demands associated with the Industrial Revolution.

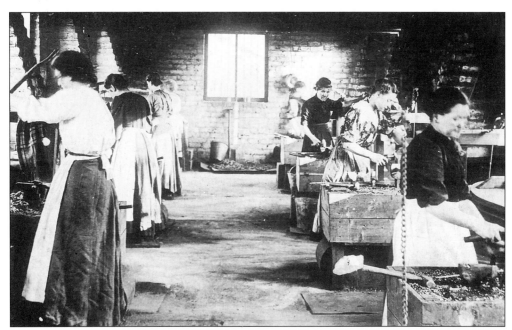

Women chainmakers employed by Adam Hill at his Butterworth Hall smithy in Milnrow, c.1884. Working in the metal trades was not uncommon for women in the earlier years of the nineteenth century. Directories show Elizabeth Healey working as a blacksmith in 1818, while Elizabeth Skelern carried on her husband's trade as tinman and brazier after his death in 1813.

John William Meeks, pictured at his smithy in Wardle during June 1950: still a working blacksmith at the age of 90.

Labourers employed to paint the gas holders in 1907. Rochdale's police commissioners bought the Rochdale Gas Light and Coke Company in 1844 for the sum of £26,000. Fourteen years later there were 7,227 consumers, paying 4/- (20p) per 1,000 cubic feet. Increasing demands for gas led to several extensions, culminating in a complete remodelling and enlargement of the works in 1871 under the direction of Samuel Hunter, the new manager. The cost of the venture was some £70,000, with further expense in 1878 when the building of Dane Street caused alterations to the approach. By 1907, when local production of gas was around 385 million cubic feet annually, the price to consumers had shrunk to 2/8d (12p) per 1,000 cubic feet.

Constructing the new canal bridge at Firgrove in July 1907: another of the civil engineering projects which were a feature of the town's development at the turn of the century, creating work for many.

Clifford Ashton's photograph of Sarah Heyworth 'knocking-up' the workers of Franchise Street in April 1934. Better than an alarm clock, because they couldn't be switched off, 'knockers-up' rattled on the bedroom windows of their client's houses with a pole topped by umbrella wires, stopping only when they saw the curtains twitch.

Littleborough's lamplighter at work outside the Central School around 1910.

Henry Whittle, on the left, with his van fleet outside the bakery at Littleborough, c.1921. Harry Smith, known as Big Harry, leans against the first van with Sim Shaw at the third van from the left. Legend has it that Henry built up the trade from his bakery shop, opened at Featherstall in 1893, by trundling loaves around in a wheelbarrow for door-to-door sales.

Mixing the dough at Whittle's Bakery, Littleborough, photographed by T. Harvey, c.1970. Once mixed, the dough was left to prove in the large tubs before being portioned up and baked.

Once baked, the loaves were tipped out of their tins and placed on racks for cooling before slicing, wrapping and despatch.

Inside the fractionation plant where fatty acids were split at the Armour Hess chemical works, now Akzo Chemie, Hollingworth Road, Littleborough, c.1955.

Five

At Your Service

Herbert Milne's butchers stall on the corner of the old market on Lord Street around 1910, with not a refrigerator in sight!

Chemists selling cutprice patent medicines are nothing new. John Taylor advertised the sale of 'patent medicines at reduced prices' on his shop front in 1895. His apprentice, J. Fielden, stands in the doorway with the usual contingent of children attracted by the presence of a camera on either side of the shop.

Medicine bottle label, c.1930. Dispensing chemists produced and labelled their own preparations for minor ailments. Olive oil and raspberry vinegar was a popular remedy for coughs and colds.

Purity JS Mark

Olive Oil

AND

Raspberry Vinegar.

*Prepared from
the Fresh Ripe Fruits.*

DOSE.
A tea-spoonful to a dessert-spoonful.

J. SLATTERY, M.P.S.,
Dispensing Chemist,
405, Halifax Road, Smallbridge,
ROCHDALE.

The Pioneers' Central Store, decorated for Rochdale's Municipal Jubilee in 1906. Standing on the corner of Toad Lane and St Mary's Gate, the store was built in 1864, a mere twenty years after the Pioneers started trading.

Smallbridge's 'Blue Co-op', run by the Conservative Co-operative Society at No. 407 Halifax Road, c.1890.

Staff at the Co-op's Albion Road Laundry, Rochdale, in 1931. Mrs Kennedy at the front in the patterned dress, recalls 12 hour shifts, starting at 7.30 am when she was 14 years old in 1917. Her wages were 11/- (52p) for a 6 day week.

Banish the Drudgery
of the old-fashioned washing day at home by using our

Family Wash Service

A POSTCARD OR 'PHONE CALL

BRINGS US TO YOUR DOOR.

and YOU SAVE THE DIVIDEND.

CO-OPERATIVE
Laundry and Dry Cleaning Works

Norman Road :: Rochdale
TELEPHONE - 3367.

A phonecall or even just a postcard could secure the Co-op's door-to-door delivery services for laundry and dry cleaning in 1936.

Holden Ward, Rochdale Infirmary, shortly after opening in 1897. Notice the child in the second bed on the right; the children's ward must have been full. Thomas Watson donated the funds for the hospital in 1883 when there were thirty eight beds, with separate wards for men and women and smaller units for children and 'special' diseases.

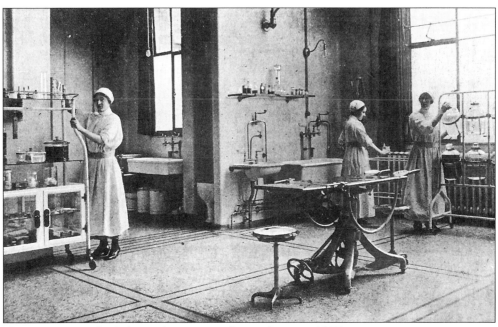

Nurses preparing the Infirmary's operating theatre for use, c.1917.

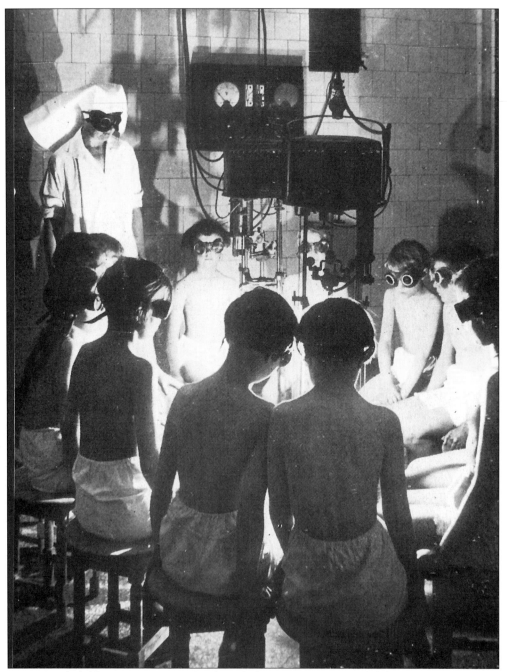

A group of children receiving artificial sunlight treatment at Rochdale Infirmary in 1928. During that year a total of 23,153 treatments were recorded, including regular treatment for children attending Rochdale's 'open air' school at Brownhill.

Dearnley Union Workhouse, Union Road, 1890. Opened in December 1877, the institution replaced former township workhouses as the destination of the poor and needy. Eventually it became part of the Birch Hill Hospital complex.

Residential nursery at the institution, before it became part of the general hospital, c.1948. Babies and children of up to 5 years old could be cared for if their parents were ill or unable to provide a home for their children.

Springfield Maternity and Child Welfare Home, c.1920. Springfield House was built in 1866 by James Davenport, head of the Globe Machine Works and was initially purchased by the Council for use as a TB sanatorium. However, in 1918 the Council decided to establish the Maternity and Child Welfare Home at Springfield, duly appointing Miss E. Prince as temporary matron at a salary of £70 per annum. Maternity charges were fixed at £2, with infant care charges of 7/6 (35p) per week, reduced in cases of need. Children of up to 2 years old were generally admitted for care with an upper limit of 5 years in exceptional circumstances. The Maternity Home closed in September 1930, following an outbreak of puerperal fever, but by that time there was a municipal midwifery service, employing ten domiciliary midwives to supervise home confinements as well as Birch Hill Hospital, which had begun to offer maternity care under the Local Government Act of 1929.

Pupils pose for a class photograph with their teacher and headmaster at Newbold School on Vavasour Street, c.1918. Teaching was considered a suitable profession for young women, although they had to finish if they married. Newbold School opened on 8 November 1886, was enlarged in 1896 and again in 1902.

Newhey Council School's basketball team, pictured with their teachers in 1914. After-school-hours coaching for team games was all part of the working day for teachers.

Electric House, Rochdale, c.1951 as seen in W.T. Carter's outstanding photograph. The Electric House on Smith Street was built by R. and T. Howarth to house the electricity showrooms, offices and domestic appliance sales outlet under one roof. The showrooms were officially opened on Monday 15 December 1930 at a time when the Borough Council was responsible for the distribution of electricity supplies throughout the town.

Rochdale Reference Library following refurbishment, c.1955.

Outside Castleton Police Station, c.1919. Police Sergeant G.W. Ridding with Police Constables Nos 32, 52, 54 and 62. The men in the trilby hats were all special constables.

This dapper looking quartet were all detectives with the Rochdale Borough Force in 1875.

Interior of Alfred Street Fire Station, off Smith Street, in 1905. Opened in 1893, the station housed two horse drawn steam fire engines, one hose tender, a dogcart escape with a ladder and a horse drawn ambulance, each fitted with a special swinging harness for quick turnouts. Six horses were stabled at the station, which was manned by police-firemen. Matthew Smith, the Brigade's assistant engineer for twenty three years, is seated on the left hand engine.

Trying on a Robert's Smoke Helmet, c.1905. This was an early form of breathing apparatus used by brigades.

Rochdale Ambulance Service, c.1942. During the Second World War women were employed for the first time as ambulance drivers in Rochdale. Based at Lea Hall, now known as the Broadwater Centre, they worked a three shift system, including nights and received basic training in midwifery and vehicle maintenance.

Inside the sorting office at Rochdale Post Office, c.1900. At that time the post office stood next to the Central Hotel in the Town Hall Square in the building occupied nowadays by the County Court.

Four men in a bucket! Watergrove Reservoir under construction, c.1935. Alderman Dearden, second from left in the bucket, descends the dam wall with his colleagues to inspect progress. By 1935 the scheme was providing much needed work for 550 previously unemployed men.

Workmen from Rochdale Corporation Transport Department pictured on Lord Street around 1920.

Coopers, employed by the council in 1924, seen here making the pails which were used for both tub lavatories and the collection of offal.

Rochdale Cleansing Department's entry for the 1931 Trades Procession, obviously hoping to prick the consciences of the town's litterbugs. The carter was Thomas Shaw.

Please! DON'T LITTER THE STREETS.

EACH YEAR
WE COLLECT...
1½ MILLION BINS
OR 22000 TONS
OF REFUSE
FROM 33,000 HOUSES

AND SALVAGE...
800 TONS OF TINS
450 TONS OF PAPER
100 TONS SCRAP METAL
1500 TONS FUEL CINDERS
40 TONS FERTILISER
30 TONS OF RAGS

ROCHDALE   CORPORATION
CLEANSING   DEPARTMENT

Rochdale Cleansing Department's entry in the 1956 Trades Procession. In 1937 the council invested in a refuse disposal plant which enabled them to reclaim all marketable salvage, including bottles, tins, paper, bones and textiles. Recycling proved to be a 'nice little earner' until the plant burned down in the 1960s.

Rochdale's street lighting maintenance gang pictured here with their platform, c.1925.

Six
Time to Spare

Paddling in Hollingworth Lake, c.1920.

Members of the Tweedale family pictured at the foot of the Healey Dell Viaduct in 1867. Healey Dell, now a Nature Reserve, remains popular with visitors.

Visitors gathered in Falinge Park in on 30 July 1907 to watch a display of Highland dancing by the Gordon Highlanders. Earlier in the month they had been entertained by the band of the Lifeguards.

Summer outing on the canal, c.1905. Boat trips on the canal were always popular. This group of Rechabites, a Temperence Society, are embarking at Littleborough.

Mock wedding concert, Watergrove United Methodist church, c.1920. Before the advent of television people enjoyed making their own entertainment and joining in the fun of putting on a concert.

Katherine Scott listening to the family phonograph at Stubley New Hall in 1900.

Robert and Ada Scott, Katherine's parents, enjoying a game of billiards in their home, c.1900.

Munitions works band, c.1918. Brass bands have been part of Lancashire's musical tradition since the mid nineteenth century, providing relaxation and enjoyment to both players and audiences. This group of munitions workers in Rochdale are depicted with their apparently much depleted band in 1918, possibly celebrating the cessation of hostilities. They are believed to be employees of Butterworth's Vale Brassworks on Ramsay Street.

Milnrow Public Band, pictured at Cliffe House, Milnrow, following their success in winning the Warrington Concert in 1930.

Noitavlas Jazz Band, c.1919. Formerly known as Temple Street Jazz Band, the group's more unusual name is the backward spelling of salvation due to the fact that they used to meet at the back of the Salvation Army Citadel on Lord Street. Like many other Carnival Jazz Bands of the period, Noitavlas played their music as they paraded through the streets. Their main instrument was a kazoo, a kind of flattened tube, open at each end, through which the player hummed a tune. The band was started by the man seated in the middle of the front row, a Mr Collins, who also had a fairground ride opposite the Hippodrome. The youngsters on the front row, starting second from the left, were Bob Greenwood, Jim Phillips, Jack Dignum, George Spencer and David Mulleeny. On 16 September 1933 over twenty Carnival Jazz Bands played in Rochdale's Trades Procession with the ensuing competition being won by the Dinkie Band from Oldham.

Fun on the paddle boats at Hollingworth Lake, c.1920. Originally built in 1800 as a feeder reservoir for the Rochdale Canal, the lake soon became a favourite destination for local people in their sparse and precious leisure time. With the advent of railways, visitors from further afield headed for its attractions too. Hostelries sprang up, boating became a favourite pastime, vying with strolling around the lake, and you could even dance on an open air dancing stage or indoors at the Public Hall on Lake Bank if the weather was poor. Little wonder that Hollingworth Lake, now part of a large country park, acquired the nickname of 'th'Weighver's Seaport.'

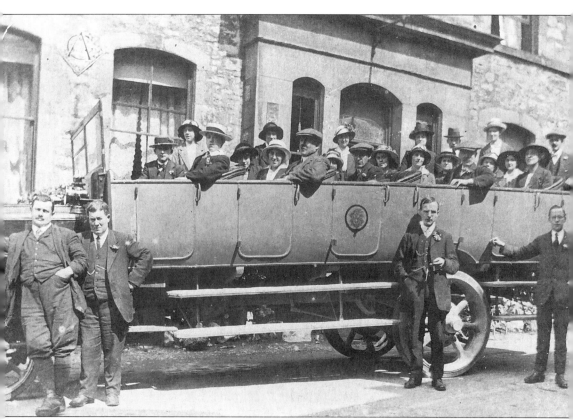

Greenoff's Coaches, c.1912. The advent of the motorcoach, or chara (charabanc), as it was more fondly known, gave thousands of people the chance to take cheap day trips to the sea or countryside. Works outings, school trips and church groups all climbed aboard the local 'bone shakers' to experience the novel freedom of travel for pleasure. In this picture Arthur Greenoff is seen on the extreme left, leaning against the engine of one of his coaches. He and his partner, Cyril Shaw, were amongst Rochdale's earliest coach owners, offering week long trips to Torquay by 1913. In those days each row of seats had separate doors, reached from double running boards slung along the length of the vehicle. (See also p. 64).

Children in rock pools, bathing huts, boats and sunshades, c.1890. With the advent of railway and later coach travel, more and more people began to spend their annual holidays, known then to most Rochdalians as Wakes Week, at seaside resorts such as Blackpool. This image is from the Leach Tweedale archive, and is probably of an east coast resort.

Visiting the seaside for the day, c.1925, is Mrs Sidebottom with her children Alma and Sam.

Rochdale Amusement Managers' Association lined up outside the Central Hotel in the Town Hall Square on 21 September 1919. It seems hard to believe that these sombrely clad men were in charge of the town's fun! John Jackson, director of the Hippodrome and Empire, is seated on the front row, third from the left, with Norman Robinson of the Theatre Royal third from the right. Harry P. Fortune of the Queens Cinema, Littleborough, stands on the extreme right of the back row, with Fred Kay of the Palace Cinema (now Xanadu's) standing third from the right. By 1941 the Jackson family controlled the Hippodrome, Empire, Ceylon Picture Palace and Rialto Super Cinema, which boasted a cafe in addition to its screen.

Opposite: Theatre Royal playbill, 1855. Rochdale's original Theatre Royal stood on Toad Lane, housed in a building which had formerly been a Wesleyan chapel. It was knocked down in 1865 to make way for the Pioneers' Central Store and in 1867 a new theatre, initially called the Prince of Wales, was built on Manchester Road. Later to be renamed the Theatre Royal, this theatre burned down on 24 November 1954. Sharing the bill on that fateful night were Tessie O'Shea and Semprini, whose piano was salvaged by the fire brigade.

THEATRE ROYAL

ROCHDALE,

TWO NIGHTS ONLY

MONDAY and TUESDAY, MARCH 5th and 6th, 1855,

THE CELEBRATED

CHINESE

JUGGLERS!

The troupe that appeared at the Theatre Royal, Drury-lane, in the Spring of 1854,
and who have just returned from a successful tour in France.

PROGRAMME--PART 1.

Mons. BENEFF with his Wonderful Ball.
Mons. RENEFF in his extraordinary Herculean Feats.

After which the

CHINESE JUGGLERS

Circus and Hippodrome, Newgate, c.1908. 'Th'owd Circus' opened on 29 October 1883, mainly as a venue for music hall acts, but on 20 January 1903 showed the first animated pictures to be seen in Rochdale. This view gives a clear idea of its location, with the Town Hall visible behind. The Circus closed in May 1908 when the Jackson family demolished it to make way for the Hippodrome, a modern music hall, which they opened six months later on 16 November 1908.

Rochdale Hippodrome, decorated for the visit of King George V and Queen Mary in July 1913.

Definitely not a flea pit! The Regal Cinema opened on 16 May 1938 with a Barbara Stanwyk film called *Stella Dallas*. In later years it became first an ABC, then a Canon Cinema, but sadly, in 1995 falling audience figures finally resulted in closure and the building, now renamed The Ritz, is operating as a bingo hall.

Jock McAvoy, known as the Rochdale Thunderbolt, whose tremendous punching power won him three Lonsdale Belts and pulled in the crowds, c.1930.

Off for a spin in 1910! Rochdale Cycling Club met up outside the Central Hotel, which stood to the left of the Empire Hall in the Town Hall Square.

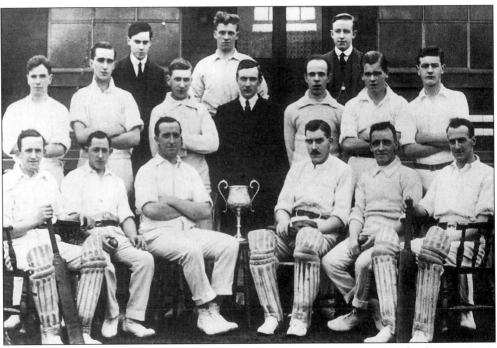

Milnrow Cricket Club's Second XI were League Cup winners in 1922. J. Holt, the captain, is seated on the front row, to the left of the cup.

Smallbridge Rugby Football Club's team photograph, around 1923.

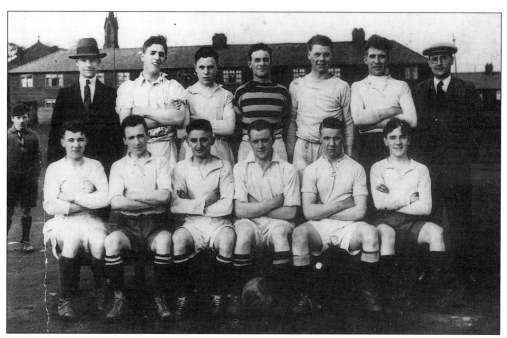

Amateur football teams included various tradesmen's groups, like this team, the Rochdale Butchers, photographed in the early 1920s.

Clifford Ashton's lively image of the Norden Riviera in 1935. Facilities at the Riviera included badminton, horse riding and dancing plus sun bathing in season! A tea garden provided refreshments for patrons and many have regretted its closure in 1966.

Carnival time in 1956. Leonard Wild's snapshot captures the air of excitement as carnival floats travel along St Mary's Gate in Rochdale's Jubilee Year, when the town celebrated the centenary of its incorporation as a Borough.

Opposite: Members of Rochdale CHA Rambling Club, walking in the Pendle area in 1955. Founded in 1904 by T. H. Butterworth, the club is still going strong having celebrated its ninetieth anniversary in 1994.

All the fun of the fair! Again, in 1956, Leonard Wild's photograph catches the glitz and tinsel glamour of the travelling fair's visit to Rochdale in the Jubilee Year. At that time funfairs were still held on the Holme, which had been the site of the cattle markets until 1951. It is now the site of the police station.

Another fairground scene from 1956. For a modest outlay of 1/- (5p), punters could visit the burlesque tent and see Suzzarde, Mistress of Allure, in Stance of the Artistic, plus the Dance of the Seven Veils and a sword swallower! Quite exotic fare for Rochdale in 1956 and certainly value for money!

Seven
Getting About

Herbert Bright with his 6 hp Daimler in 1901.

Early travel was by foot or by horse. Mary Alice Hartley, known as Ailse O'Fussars, was the last of Rochdale's 'Lime Gal' drivers. At one time she ran a string of about twenty 'Gals' (Galloway ponies) carrying coal from Shawforth and sometimes lime from Burnley or Clitheroe. Here she is pictured in later life with Gerry, her beloved donkey.

TODMORDEN TURNPIKE ROADS
STEANOR BOTTOM BAR

Tolls to be taken at this Bar under the Local Act: 1st & 2nd Geo. 4. cap. III.

	s	d
For every Horse or other Beast drawing any such, Berlin, Landau, Chariot, Chaise, Chair, Curricle, Cloash-Honse, Litter, or other such, Carriage the sum of	0	7
For every Horse or other Beast drawing any Waggon or other such four-wheeled Carriage or any Cart or other such two-wheeled Carriage, with wheels of the breadth of six inches, or upwards, at the bottom or sole thereof the sum of	0	5
For every Horse or other Beast drawing any Waggon, Train, Cart, or other such Carriage, with wheels of the breadth of four and a half inches, and less than six inches at the bottom, or not over to be such of	0	6
For every Horse or other Beast drawing any Waggon or other such four-wheeled Carriage or any Carriage, other under four and a half on the bottom or sole thereof. The sum of —	0	7
For every Horse or other Beast drawing any other, or other four-wheeled Carriage or any Cart or other such two-wheeled Carriage with wheels of the breadth than three inches, the sum of	0	9
For every Horse, Wheeled And laden, or this, and not drawing, the sum of	0	2
For every other Horse or of the Sum of	0	½
For every Calf, Sheep, Swine or lamb, the Sum of	0	¼

N.B. The above Tolls to be taken for the first, fifth, and eighth times of passing respectively in one day, but not for repassing through the same, and such Tolls not to be payable more than three times in one day at the same Toll Gate

Exemptions from the above Tolls as mentioned in the local and General Turnpike

This Bar is a Ticket Bar to and from Wadsworth Mill Bar

J.P. & W. SUTCLIFFE.
Clerks ... and Trustees

Tolls levied on travellers at the Steanor Bottom Toll Bar on the Todmorden Turnpike, c.1821.

Toll Bar at Half Acre, Brimrod, in 1907. The houses, standing on what is now Roch Valley Way, are still occupied.

Bacup's horse drawn omnibus, pictured outside the Spread Eagle on Cheetham Street, c.1900. In 1818 the Enterprise market coach ran between the Spread Eagle and the York Inn at Shude Hill, Manchester, on every Tuesday, Thursday and Saturday, departing from Rochdale at 7 am and returning at 7 pm.

Laying tramlines at Spotland Bridge in 1902. Early trams were hauled by steam engines, (see the picture of Drake Street on p. 16).

Ready for off! The Littleborough tram, parked over the maintenance pit at Mellor Street tramsheds, c.1905.

Crowds turned out at Summit to greet the first electric tramcar on the Rochdale, Littleborough, Summit run on 10 August 1905. Maybe the youngsters anticipated speedier, cheaper travel to Rochdale, with the delights of animated pictures to be sampled at 'Th'owd Circus.'

Taking up the tramlines, c.1933. Workmen taking a well earned rest outside the Exchange Hotel on Featherstall Road, Littleborough.

A Rochdale Corporation double decker, photographed outside the Mellor Street Depot with the last electric tram, c.1930.

Motorised commercial transport, c.1918. The acquisition of motorised vehicles was a milestone for most firms, often marked by a staff photograph similar to this one showing the first motor lorry owned by the Lowfield Spinning Company at Firgrove.

Holt Brothers' Removals, c.1915. Holt Brothers, later to become the Yelloway coaching firm, were carriers and furniture removers in their early days. This solid wheeled wagon, pictured outside their Fishwick Street premises, was chain driven.

Ellen Smith's coach station and garage at Heybrook in 1925. Whit Week trips to Blackpool are advertised in the window, possibly in their first purpose built coach, acquired in 1924, an Albion Viking eighteen seater with a full set of pneumatic tyres to guarantee comfort.

Barges passing Clegg Hall in 1920. After opening on 21 December 1804, Rochdale Canal provided a commercial route between Lancashire and Yorkshire for almost 150 years, finally closing to traffic in 1952. Plans to reopen its thirty three miles of waterway for recreational purposes hinge on the Millenium Project.

Castleton Canal Bridge, prior to widening in 1927, showing the locks and lock-keeper's house, tenanted by a greengrocer by that time.

Rochdale Canal Basin, taken from Richard Street in 1935, showing warehousing, the Canal Company Offices and timber in Fletcher Bolton's canalside yard.

Summit Tunnel repair gang, c.1900. George Stephenson built the Manchester to Leeds railway which opened on 1 March 1841. At that time, Summit Tunnel, 2,869 yards long, was the longest railway tunnel ever built, representing tremendous feats of engineering and logistics by the contractor, John Stevenson, and sheer hard work by the navvies who dug it out.

Rochdale Station pictured in 1910, had twin long-island platforms, both with double bays at each end, the whole of which were covered over with glass canopies supported by airy cast iron columns and roofing spars. Opened in 1889, it replaced the earlier station which had been built some fifty yards away, near Oldham Road, in 1839.

Heading for Rochdale and beyond: a steam train passing through Littleborough Station, around 1902.

Eight
Pennine Edges

Nichol's Teashop and Public Hall, Lake Bank, Hollingworth Lake, c.1905.

Buckley Hill Lane, Milnrow, c.1910. Workmen taking a break from their task of resurfacing the cobbled lane with tarmac, using what appears to be a combined steamroller and tar boiler.

Ladyhouse Farm and Fold, pictured around 1910, were demolished to make way for the M62 motorway.

A group of children outside the Plough Inn at Ladyhouse, Milnrow, in 1907. The baby, who is barefoot, appears to be tied to the chair as a safety precaution.

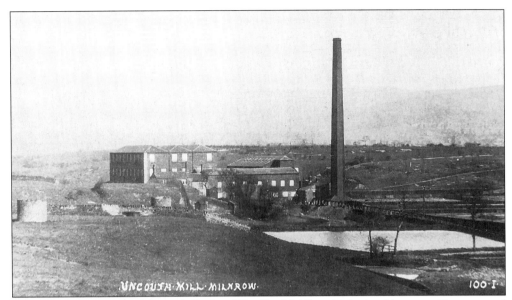

John Smith's prosperous Uncouth Bridge (Woollen) Mills, which stood between Firgrove and Wildhouse, c.1905. Milnrow's sewage works were built close by in 1897 and in the foreground are airshafts from the former Belfield Colliery workings.

Dale Street, Milnrow, photographed by Thomas Pinder in 1910. In the background the imposing bulk of the Milnrow Spinning Company's mill rears above the much older three storey weaver's cottages.

Residents, local children and a dog faced the camera on Entwistle Street, Milnrow in 1900. This view is looking towards the bottom of Buckley Hill Lane.

Milnrow and Newhey Agricultural Show in 1919. Abraham Fielding, President of the Society is presenting a special award to the owner of the champion heifer. Harbour Lane and Ladyhouse can be seen in the background.

Shaw's milkfloat on Huddersfield Road at Newhey, c.1900.

Clegg Hall, c.1865 which dates from around the beginning of the seventeenth century, and was probably built for Theophilus Ashton, who sold it to his brother in law, Edmund Howorth, in 1618, for £1500. Between 1818 and 1869 Clegg Hall became a public house, known at one time as the 'Black Sloven' to commemorate a very speedy horse owned by Charles Turner, who lived at the hall in the eighteenth century.

Littleborough Cycle Parade in 1911, the Coronation year of King George V and Queen Mary, whose images stare out from the flag above the pony cart. Leslie Scott, a skilled amateur whose father was a local millowner, took this photograph.

A proud pigeon fancier driving his mobile display aviary in the 1911 parade, seen through the lens of Leslie Scott.

Harehill Road, Littleborough, c.1910. Looking up the road towards the Co-operative building, on the right, with its distinctively domed roof. The tall chimney on the left belonged to Littleborough gas works. Leading the procession of traffic coming down the middle of the road is a parcel delivery handcart, heading back to the railway station, while the only motor vehicle in sight trundles sedately behind the horse and carriage! On opposite corners of Harehill Road and Victoria Street were Hallett's boot and shoemakers shop, on the left, with William Clough's butchers shop on the right.

Church Street, Littleborough, c.1903. Boasting a full wall of enamelled advertising plates, Robert Hall's grocery store stood on the corner of Church Street and Harehill Road.

J.C. Crossley, mineral water manufacturer, Littleborough, c.1912. Crossley's delivery wagon, with the horse decked out in plumes and brasses, may have been heading for the Cycle Parade. In 1885 Crossleys were operating from Morgan Street where they produced soda water and gingerbeer but by 1907 they had removed to Charles Street.

Ealees and Durn, with Oak Street in the foreground, c.1910. Uber Mill, in the centre of the picture, housed the Victoria Dyeing, Raising and Finishing Company. In 1916, when the mill was burned down, part of it collapsed onto Frankfort Cottage. Frankfort Mill stands across Halifax Road between the canal and railway. It was owned by W. Barker Ltd in 1910, producing cotton drills, satins and sheetings but during the depression of the 1930s it closed down and the area is now used as a scrapyard. Durn Foundry can be seen to the right of the mills; in front of it is the Durn branch of the Littleborough Co-op, opened in 1906.

The Rake Inn, Blackstone Edge Old
Road, Littleborough, c.1907. Used as a
coaching inn since 1696, the Rake is said
to have provided a change of horses for
stage coaches, prior to their long haul up
Blackstone Edge. During the Second
World War the celler was used by a local
contingent of the Home Guard. Windy
Bank, on the hill behind the Rake, was
built by John Butterworth in 1635.

'Owd Caleb' of Benthouse,
Littleborough, c.1905. Housewives in the
area were guaranteed fresh poultry by
'Owd Caleb' who transported his live
birds around in a sack. Customers chose
a bird and Caleb completed his sale by
wringing the victim's neck.

Rough Farm and the Oil Mill, Blackstone Edge Old Road, Littleborough, c.1905. Built as a fulling mill, the Oil Mill was originally called Holehouse Mill but time and dialect combined to corrupt the name. High Peak cottages stand on the site today, named after the Derbyshire constituency of Sir Alfred Law, the owner of Lydgate and Durn Mills, who built them.

Razing the chimney at New Mill, Littleborough on 24 August 1906.

Floods at Rock Nook, Summit, in February 1910. This view looks towards Todmorden with Fothergill and Harvey's Rock Nook Mill on the right.

Infants from St James' Church of England School, Wardle, with their teacher and headmaster in April 1914.

Thomas Dearden, greengrocer and carrier of Dean Street, Wardle, selling produce from the back of his cart around 1910.

Wardle's first motorbus waiting in the square in 1927.

Wardle Agricultural Fair, c.1907. Shows and fairs were an important part of the agricultural year, attracting large numbers of visitors and participants. In 1900 Rochdale was the venue for the legendary Royal Lancashire Agricultural Society Show which ran over three days in July. Classes for entries were limited to residents of Lancashire and typically included livestock: cattle, sheep, pigs and horses as well as poultry, dogs, pigeons, dairy produce, honey and eggs. Prizes ranged from 5/- (25p) as third prize for honey to £20 for a shire horse.

Working horses on Thimble Hall Farm at Wardle which was tenanted by James Crossley in 1900.

Watergrove Village, c.1930. The hamlet of Watergrove, with its United Methodist Free Church dating from 1857, and its cotton mill, built by John Stott and Company in 1881, was soon to be drowned beneath a new reservoir for Rochdale.